The Palace of

Contemplating Departure

The Palace of Contemplating Departure

poems by

Brynn Saito

Red Hen Press | Pasadena, CA

The Palace of Contemplating Departure

Copyright © 2013 by Brynn Saito

All Rights Reserved

Book design by Mark E. Cull

Book layout by Jennifer Hawley and Skyler Schulze

ISBN 978-1-59709-716-1 (tradepaper)

ISBN 978-1-59709-677-5 (clothbound)

Library of Congress Cataloging-in-Publication Data

Saito, Brynn, 1981–

The palace of contemplating departure : poems / by Brynn Saito. —1st ed.

p. cm.

I. Title.

PS3619.A3987P35 2013

811'.6—dc23

2012029761

This publication was supported in part by an award from the National Endowment for the Arts and the generosity of Red Hen Press board member M.C. Sungaila. The Los Angeles County Arts Commission, the Los Angeles Department of Cultural Affairs, the City of Pasadena Cultural Affairs Division, Sony Pictures Entertainment, and the Dwight Stuart Youth Fund partially support Red Hen Press.

First Edition

Published by Red Hen Press

www.redhen.org

Acknowledgments

Some of these poems have appeared in the following publications, to whose editors grateful acknowledgment is made:

Askew, "Waiting"; *Catamaran Literary Reader*, "The Exile"; *The Collagist*, "Tree of Life" (previously titled "17 Again"); *Copper Nickel*, "Winter in Denmark"; *Drunken Boat*, "The Palace of Contemplating Departure"; *The Forest Drive* (chapbook, Lettre Sauvage Press), "California Heartland"; *Harpur Palate*, "Trembling on the Brink of a Mesquite Tree"; *Hayden's Ferry Review*, "Present In All Things"; *Here is a Pen* (chapbook, Achiote Press), "A Photograph is an Argument"; *Hyphen Magazine*, "Alma, 1942"; *Mission At Tenth*, "Prayer for the One Who Could Not Stop Looking," "The Gathering Mind," and "Autumn in the Garden With Her Ghost"; *Ninth Letter*, "Spring, San Francisco" (previously titled "Match"); *Pleiades*, "Tuesday, 2 A.M."; *Third Coast*, "Shape of Fire"; *Tongue*, "Women and Children"; *Verse Daily*, "Trembling on the Brink of a Mesquite Tree"; and *Waccamaw*, "Mercy Me."

Poets 11, 2010: An Anthology of Poems (San Francisco Public Library), "Trembling on the Brink of a Mesquite Tree," "Daughter," and "Tuesday, 2 A.M."

My deepest thanks to the Kundiman Asian American Poetry Fellowship, A Gathering of the Tribes and the Key West Literary Seminar, whose gracious support contributed to the writing of the manuscript. Heartfelt gratitude to Traci Brimhall, Tina Chang, Marie Howe, Suzanne Gardinier, Valarie Kaur, Gabriel Galindo, Nicholas Jahr, Kris Brandenburger, and Cindy Shearer, whose close reading, mentorship, and guidance helped bring the book into fruition. For the sustaining friendship of Susie, Susan, Karen, Ellen, Eleanor, Lisa, Sekayi, and Laura, I'm forever grateful. To the sustaining grace and strength of Marilyn Oh, I'm beholden. And many thanks to David Mason, for believing in the manuscript, and to everyone at Red Hen Press, who helped make the book possible.

Lastly, boundless love and appreciation to my family, especially my mother and father, whose stories are in these pages.

For Leigh

In the middle of a field
with nothing to cling to
a skylark sings
                    —Basho

Contents

III. Shape of Fire

IV. Steel and Light

The Palace of

Contemplating Departure

I. Ruined Cities

First Incarnation

According to Theresa I was born from a wolf.
I prowled the moor for many ages
singed from the inside by my own lust.
When I met you in autumn
you were sitting on the trunk of a conifer
crowned with bluets. You said
There's a pack of dogs inside me
threatening to eat its leader who is wounded.
I said *Let them.* You've always wanted
to go to God as a child approaches a wolf
in a ruined city. So I took your palm,
pressed it to my chest, and the sky inside me
widened. Now the night slips me her best skin
and my mouth takes no prisoners.

Tuesday, 2 A.M.

Then the monk became a hawk and the hawk became a clown
who counted on an abacus
the innocent dead

and I woke in my America
and read about the boy
who was killed while I was sleeping. He didn't have a gun—

he was brandishing a hairbrush—
but the cops thought he did
so they shot twenty times.

Right before I woke
the clown became a phone and the phone was the old kind
with holes for a dial and it didn't stop ringing
even when retrieved.

My country is the child
who squirms in her stroller in a stalled subway car.
My country is the wet piece

of sweet-flavored plastic
put inside the child's mouth to silence her surge.
I am a waker, blistered by morning

who, right before the ringing, was dreaming of a heart
surrounded by pistols
and the pistols pointed outward
and the muscle pumped blood.

TREMBLING ON THE BRINK OF A MESQUITE TREE

And the Lord said *Surprise me* so I moved to LA.
After packing my posters and scrubbing the bathroom and bidding goodbye
to the permanent circus, I drove through The South

with its womb-like weather, and I drove through the center
with its cross-hatched streams, and the century unspooled
like a wide, white road with lines for new writing

and the century unspooled like a spider's insides.
The country was a cipher, so I voted my conscience.
The country was a carton of ten rotten eggs.

The country was a savior—come deliver us from evil!—
and my car burned a scar across the back of an angel
and yes, I was afraid. No I've never gone hungry but I've woken alone

with a ghost in my throat and I've been like the child
who's sure she perceives some creature in the dark—
some night-breathing thing—and I know there is something I can almost see . . .

But the future's a bright coin spinning in sunlight
so fast that it's sparking a flame in the grass, and who knows
where they'll find me—on which sunken highway?—so I'm writing this poem

to remember my name. I'm writing this poem
to let something go, in the mode of surrender, since God
needs a ritual, like kissing needs another, or a knife needs the softness

of a melon in summer, and leaving New York is like leaving
the circus, and entering America is like entering a fortress
flooded by soda and we float to the bars in our giggling terror

and driving from one shore across to another?
That's one sign for freedom, one small stab at change
so when the Lord said *Surprise me* I moved to LA.

City In Which I Love

Spring Street 6

When the last bomb dog snarls and sniffs
when he nicks your black sack and you fail to grasp
the hidden weight of such random acts, let this
be a sign: the last branch has fallen from the root-sprout.
Embrace the tamed beast as your long lost brother.
Crawl in his gut and sleep like the child
who sucks through the night on his own broken thumb.

4th Floor Walk-Up

His desire's dying in the November half-light
of their Harlem apartment. Hers is the blade
of a rusted scissor. When it snows over slate
she ghosts over scenery, slips through their kitchen
without touching a thing, dreams herself forms
to inhabit then smashes their six free teacups,
a thousand dull knives, a TV signal that comes to them
sometimes. Although they fight, his body still turns
to hers in the night: two shells clicking on a frameless
mattress, four arms missing the reckless sea.

East 3rd

Summer comes, my sister visits, and a corner bar kicks us
to the hard-knocked curb. We're two bright beasts
wrapped around each other's necks like head-locked
monkeys in a broken crib. East Third Street jingles
with bent plants descending from brick-backed lattice
and black-eyed railings: they take hits from stubbed cigarettes
at four a.m. Her spine in the night curls the bed sheets
like a question. She's come to get even. I see that this city
can summon her demons: the liquor and tinsel and smoke-dust
around her make a home for the war she wages within.

Chambers

Somewhere in the ache, in the hungry beginning
you moved here to cash in your fittest hand.
But the city folded. So hot to turn a profit
it ate itself gladly. Soon two searchlights soared:
they scraped over heaven. They roughed up the witness
for hints of a language. They burned through the ice film
coating tree-lined streets. Soot-filled water oozed
through sidewalk. The first warm breeze came coasting
down the Hudson. Each promise you made
from Second to Lex or Carmine to Houston
showed new strength: Yes, this—our life.
Now we carry the days as if they were chosen.

Leaving New York

Sunday morning on the downtown F. A puddle of vomit
coats the seat beside you. When you see it you move
to a seat by the window and the city's streets
stretch before you like small black scars
crawling towards water. You danced right there
till four in the morning. Sobered on homefries
at your local diner. Walked along the promenade
and thought of your body, its fall onto traffic, would it flail
and jump? Now copters circle, ships pull cargo
and lines of graffiti climb in the window as you sink
beneath Brooklyn, trapped as an echo. When memory rises
you know you can't hold it; you're moving to the shore
of an unknown coast. But you made the most of it.
Now the change you begged for on cold street corners comes.

A Photograph is An Argument

Did you see the soldier holding the newborn
a Dutch brigadier on the Afghan border?
I saw a picture on a Sunday morning—
page A16. It was creased by my elbow
and stained with a tea leaf. When you
heard the general make claims about rape—
how some women willed it to settle for money—
I had to dream him, the stitch of his inseam
sewn to perfection. In my dream he tied a ribbon
around a rusted machete and tilted
the tip towards that bulge in your neck.
I used to press my face there to inhale your body.
But every photograph is an argument
for believing in something without touching
or tasting it and every dream betrays the lie.

The Palace of Contemplating Departure

You wandered through my life like a backwards wish
when I was ready for deliverance.
I was ready for release

like a pinball in God's mouth
like charanga on Tuesdays
like the summer in Shanghai

when we prayed for a rainstorm,
bartered our shame, tore open oranges
with four dirty thumbs.

The forecast said Super
so we chartered a yacht
and we planted a garden on the unbending prow

but the sea said Surrender
with its arms full of salt, and wind shook the seeds
from our shirt coat pockets

so when we washed up on the shoreline of sunlight
near the city of wind
we were broken and thin, like wraiths at a wake.

But you tilted your head up and told me I was wild
so I lifted my life
and I lifted your life

and we wandered through the gate of radiant days
then we married our splendor
in the hall of bright rule.

I thank you again: you gave madness a chance
and you lassoed the morning
and we met on a Tuesday
in a dance hall in Shanghai
and I left you in a leap year for the coveted shoreline

and you wept like a book when it's pulled from a well.

But you were the one who told me I was wild
and you were the one who wrestled the angel

and I knew when I left you
that courage was a choice
and memory, a spear,
and the X of destination is etched on my iris
and shifts with the seasons—
don't think of the phoenix, think of the mountain.

But where will I go now with my tireless wonder?
And when will I again be brave like that?

The Exile

If you are the country
then I am a prisoner
cast into exile

making my way
to our shore home in dreams
then waking in the north

where stone drives me mad.
Now the world is a free thing:
formless and stark.

Tin cans everywhere.
Rain filling the tin then
spilling over.

There are no names
for this—
the charge of a river

flooding the embers
shaking free roots
of the oldest trees.

Today my grief turned
to a dream—a desire for home.
The desire filled me.

The dream itself
was its own kind of paradise—
false but perfect

bearing the details
of our wild life, the spectral lines
of a world wrung dry.

I could have waded forever
in the familiar dark
but I chose flight—

or succumbed to its leanness—
and left you in the river.
Then I leapt into lightning.

THE MESSENGER

I stood on a rock in the desert
my palms turned out like two doves
my face tilted the way a bell tilts
before it pleases with song.

Wind swept around me
like God's breath. My wings
of no use to me. My dress
the color of drowning.
I was floating away from myself
so fast I forgot what I loved.

When I was human
I used to climb the green hill
for this same pleasure.
The city of rust and smoke
slithered beneath me.
It's done: never again in my life
will I be only one thing.

Cambria, Late Spring

The last time you were beside me
it was April.
I knew it was over
but my body was equivocal.
My body was a boat
for your staggering;
my heart, a stone.
Guilt moved through me
like a sharp red rope.

Then the dream of the cypress
splitting in two.
Then the trembling sonata
moving through the promise
of minor to major
then changing again
from the son to the man.
Then a vision of the future
without your hands.

When the act was over
I heard you call out
like a sparrow in the cold dawn
to know the enemy.

AVIGNON, EARLY SUMMER

A woman

    downwind from Nagasaki now dying

      is forced to decide

    what form might hold her

when she's made into flame

      then scattered as ash.

A field, perhaps.

    Of sakura. With bright white blossoms

blooming in the dark.

    We got married in her park

      under one thousand trees

    then we took a plane

down to Avignon

    that barracked city in the south

near the sea

where men on stilts with powdered faces

made plays into the night.

No guns pushed inward on the plush spot.

No war moved closer.

When I asked: *What?* You said: *A child*—

Then the night grew warmer

and the sky, lighter before dark.

WINTER IN DENMARK

To be had by the sea. To return to the grave
but find the grave empty. Unsure about most things
related to loss, I say the body is a feast

of memory when my father-in-law ponders the scars
on my arm. He takes his two thumbs, rubs them over my hands
inspecting each mark like the doctor he is.

Such is the way of the great white Dane who tends to my skin
like rain on a valley. Now as he grips me, his inherited daughter—
whose greatest danger is the will inside her—

a clarion calls from across the shore. At midnight he listens
for his two lost sons, those thwarted princes
who died without warning. I'm their age now

despite their decade of absence. It's winter in Denmark
despite a dearth of snow. A fog falls
on the slapping bay. I'm upstairs dreaming of his two dead boys

asleep near his third one—the one who is breathing.
Jon trembles with dreams he will forget in the morning
and I run my thumb down the crest of his cheek. What is the mystery

that holds his skin together? Why did the roast taste so good
with the wine? Tonight, we danced. Then smoked under sparks
that fell from the sky. They loved life, but left it,

while something inside me fights every second, yet here
I remain. And the fighter is in me. And the future is in me.
I see that now. I turn to my husband and say it.

But it isn't the story of a woman redeemed, forgiving her demons
for throwing first stones. It's the story of the dreamer
on the road to Damascus, creating a savior from sand grains and light.

We wake in the morning, board a plane to the south.
Returning to the sea is like returning to a grave that's been shot through
with sunlight. The sea is so full, we begin to float.

Moonlight Over the Valley, Late October

How do you do it?
Once I was in love.
It devoured me.

How different
it must be for you—
you can radiate.

You can touch everything
without feeling anything.

Tonight my desire
is a chorus of dogs
barking for the coming storm.

Teach me how to orbit
that which you
will never kiss.

How to hold the earth's madness
in your cloak of light.

II. Women and Children

Cottonwood [Mother]

My children as they wandered from me took on the shapes of beauty. I was proud of the way they suffered though I know they were undone by the sharpness of the earth's asking: Do you know hunger, do you know rage, do you know the color of grief? The color of grief is the bright amber of wasted honey. It's the gunmetal gray of Savannah skies before breaking open. Look at my back. It's a map of the way the world looks when everyone is sleeping. It will show you the way to my children's stories. It will sing.

Climbing Bare Rock [First Daughter]

You and I, child, were roped from the day the coyote stole the first humans from the sea. Our twin souls, harnessed. My own mother told me I'd never be brave enough to bear a son but look at me. If I wear a mask I can bear you on my back. My mask shows the world what's within me: fury at the darkening earth; twin ears saluting in joy. Teeth like sharp wire shining. Believe me dear one: I can be both wild and bent like this. I can wait for the day when you run from me in terror.

Upright Against the Redwood [Second Daughter]

He's turned toward me but I'm turned away. What I hear in the distance is the hissing sea with its constant beginnings; I'm caught by my wish for a violent renewal. They say mystics bear the wild for years before coming to terms with it. I learned fast that my right hand pressed against my left brought no peace, brought the heart's quick chirping and the body falling sideways. Mother, how did you let Father ruin your body for our birth? What anchors me always is a man's blind desire though my task has been to transcend the world of men.

Running, River [First Daughter]

What can I do but carry my brother on my sloping back, the one chosen for his beauty? What will he become should I release him into the field scattered with thorns? In the distance, the ancestors stand watching, disguised as redwoods. They wait for me to feel his clawing. They wait for me to wade into my desire for singularity. It's true: Love makes me want to die. But what else can claim a power like that? Not even God or the demon of the death, crouched in the blackest corner with his two bright lidless eyes.

Asleep in the Mapou [Son]

Bend me oh Lord to the hungering earth. Bring me to the bed of stones and lie me there but not kindly. My dress is threaded with my lover's eyes. Tell me my destiny in a low whisper. If I can make my body as beautiful as the Mapou tree, I'll be ready to reckon with my coming from dust. Once, I watched my mother tie her hair with pins. I waited for her to cry out in pain but she never cried out. She knew the art of sharp objects against soft skin, as all women do. I lay on the bed much like this, wondering how one becomes a woman.

Indrawn Seas [Mother, Departing]

Dear ones, don't believe it. The dark devotion to carnage or the crying. Or the way the hand takes up the tool to pierce the skin for singing of a different order. You were always alone. You were never apart from the wild sea with its net of rain and its one light dimly calling but calling nonetheless to your scattershot heart. Look at my hands. I've drawn them to my chest so that they might feel the fury turning beneath the sternum. In this way I speak without torching my voice. One day you too will learn that movement is a form of sound. That silence is a kind of waiting for the fires to turn the land into something useable again.

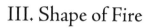

III. Shape of Fire

Second Incarnation

I come from a place of hollow pitches
made from the pull of moonlight on tongues.
Mother's body is a miracle and father's back
a map of devastations, brightly woven.
We cry together then we wander alone
like fennel seeds scattered by the wind's hand.
When I'm roving I'm weightless
like a blackened feather or a curious knife
or the woman in the photo watching the camera
and whispering her cunning into the bride's ear
which is bleeding. Freedom is the blessing
that comes from the curse of loss,
the cut heart crossing the hidden continent.
Some say everything sacred moves in a circle.
I say come closer: everything you can't imagine
is written in my eye's yellow tremor.

Mercy Me

Once when I was young my uncle took me out
to the shooting range near the eastern hills.
My cousin and I took turns
ripping up a paper target: first with a shotgun,
then with a rifle, then a semi-automatic—
that big black piece of fire that shot back
into our loose shoulders when we handled it.
It was fall in the valley and very cold.
Fog and gray light blurred the heart,
setting the mind towards a thick silence.

Yesterday the earth shook so hard
it tilted off its own axis.
I thought of the way the body kneels
before bark but only if the bark resembles
the face of God. I thought of the man
who claws for my body but only on Wednesdays
when the sky breaks open and shakes down
a black rain. I learned something about
the beautiful blue vein of seduction
that runs alongside everything deadly
on that late valley morning
when I stood beside my uncle
with a rifle in the crook of my girl arm.
We were sheltered by a family
of sycamores. They seemed dead to me
with their naked and dark-spotted bending.
They weren't dead. They were waiting.

THE GATHERING MIND

1. My father finds his father's name on the wall of internees. A museum in LA. June heat and a dry breeze. I always thought if they captured me because of my race, I'd fight back. Not like the GIs in the 442nd. But if going to war meant proving your loyalty, and doing so might free your family, then—

2. "We were helped in the shedding of dominant kinship groups by the relative individualism of the Angles and Saxons . . ."
   Tribal as prior, family as *primal*—
   But who is the "we"?

3. Thanksgiving. Auntie shows us a picture of "her sister." My own sister looks at me—a secret glance that says: *what is going on?*
   Did you know about this—
   Grandmother, we learn, gave birth too young. And the child? Sent back to Japan with a couple returning. She's a woman now, living, supposedly, in Hiroshima.

4. At a different museum: a golden copper alloy bodhisattva punctured with bullet holes.
   Art as passage—
   Art as good deed—
   Art as sacrifice, and suffering as sacrifice (versus suffering as mistake)—

5. Valarie is Sikh. Swept up with the rest during the protest, but kept longer. Held harder by the wrists for her long hair, darker skin. Later on East 3rd Street, First Avenue—that first apartment in New York—I've no idea what to do to help: make the tea, like always? Burn butter to a crisp in the blackened pan? When I finally hold her, she is laughing and crying all at once. Free and broken. And braver—

6. The construction of US citizenship occurs only when the social body is confronted with difference. Fine.

7. To destabilize the logic of the binary tree, think of the rhizome, says Deleuze. Fern, or ginger root. Overlapping lines and pointless assemblages form planes, not hierarchies, not the tree's branching into black and white, you and I.

   But how to re-intuit social reality?

8. *I cannot muster the 'we' except by finding the way in which I am tied to you. My own language must break up and yield if I am to know you.* Judith Butler. I hear she's brilliant, but at Berkeley, she's inaccessible. Don't study there, Valarie. Instead, go to where you most fear. Dine at the enemy's table, then return.

Valarie replies:

pain
penetrates
me,
drop
by
drop.

—Sappho

This is how it feels, my wrist, neck. In bed all day.

9. I reply: *Sometimes I can't resist running my fingers along a cast iron fence when walking or feeding them to the wind from a car window.*
    How to own the hate I feel for the men who harmed you—
    Ondaatje calls it the secret rehearsal, those moments before the performance. For a writer: jotting down notes in a subway car or walking through a park in winter, imagining otherwise. I'm beginning to feel the scope expanding: Everything is rehearsal, that secret part of my self always listening. The gathering mind.
    You once told me you'd be at my funeral. Or I at yours. This brought you such joy.

ALMA, 1942

To board the train without suspicion
I told the man I was Chinese
can you believe it?
You never have to lie
to survive, now do you?
So what will you do
with your curious pen
and your questions like daggers
slicing through the ripe heat
of the merciless summer,
tearing the grapes from the vine
till they drop like a satchel
of dead knuckles on dead earth?

To begin they gave us one army blanket
and one army cot,
no doors on the bathroom stalls
and no stoves for heat
only mouthfuls of dust
and the sight of a mountain
in the barbed distance
where the wind waited like a tired sniper.

Denying what you love
is like sanding your heart with a pumice stone
and the stone is on fire
and there is No Speaking Allowed Please
and No Singing.
You'll see it for yourself
when you go there roving
with your questions for the barracks
like a hungry ghost.

Daughter

One day you will find yourself on the sharpest
edge of yourself. If you're lucky

someone will answer the phone and say it's for you
and you'll come inside.

The voice is an open refuge.
Forgiveness is a tower of hands. Once when I was young

I walked through a clock then under a bridge and my whole life was lit
by a Camel cigarette. I met a man

who was not your father but he played the jazz piano so we fell into it
and let it reign. Of course

love is kind. But sometimes a person must pursue a plague
that could do some justice

to the storm within.
You'll see.

You will be thirsty too.
You will stop believing in September.

You will suddenly become aware
of the fact of your heart only when a part of it

goes missing. Well don't believe
what they tell you. No one likes change.

One day you will find yourself resisting your own waking.
Try tending to the sacred

and see where that gets you.
Try rolling through your life like a rusted train through a stockyard nation.

Nothing fills a cup like moonlight. Nothing.
No one will twist you like a man

will twist you, but that's the deal. That's how books
get written. But don't believe

what I've told you. Convince yourself.
Then burn the sage

and claw your way
through every oak on the rotting mountain.

Shape of Fire

Sometimes the fires moved closer to home
    and sometimes spun back to where they began.
        I'd hide us from the fires in a hallway closet

with a book that taught us how to talk
    with our hands: make an *a* like this, and *tomorrow*
        like this, and to make the sign for *soul*

pull an unseen string from one cupped palm.
    When we crawled from our hiding to seek out the souls
        they darted like kites through flammable sky.

Tonight I'll fly home through a wind I won't feel
    or hear through the engines to be with my sister who wept
        in my bedroom when she heard about marks

I'd made on my body. A finger to her lips
    that moves to her chest will be the sign for *tell me.*
        To tell her I'm sorry I'll take Father's saw

to the side of the highway and cut through the poles
    holding high tension lines. The things I can't live with
        exist in the soil—asleep in thistles and feasting

on seedlings. I've learned to fear the future
    like I've learned to fear the fires that burst
        in the tinder near the fallen wires.

California Heartland

People in the heartland die alone in their homes and
people like my mother inherit their dangers.
Workers like my brother wear dust coats to dinner.
They roll through the rumble and prize every fighter who
guns down flowers without waiting for a word.
I'm saying I was born in midwinter madness
when ice locked the orange trees in tendrils of freezing.
Got here gaping—two squint-eyes and slick skin—
then stabbed my way eastward for a stranger in the storm.
But the fires from the valley crossed the country like a cancer—
they ripped up the stone wheat like God knows what.
So run, I tell you, from the places that trap you
from the walls that sand you till your skin shakes down.

WAITING

I know about the waiting: keeping the phone
close to the bedside
hearing it ring

and waking, unsure
of the gathering ceiling
or the man asleep

on the bed sheets beside me.
When she finally calls me, she calls
from a strip mall

or the Santa Clara jail
or she's calling from a roadside
where four large men help heave her van upright

and I hear they're dousing fires from canyon to the coast.
Fall, says my father, *the cold front's close*
so he takes down the white lights

from the garden in the backyard—
the ones that lit our dinners
on nights we made it home.

When he huddles next to Mother
does he dream of his two daughters?
The one who took a knife

in the side of her stomach
and the one who got away?

PRAYER FOR THE ONE
WHO COULD NOT STOP LOOKING

Do you remember how the spirit
moved across the living room
and the living room took it
like a wheat field under rain
and I took you by the wrist
and said Listen: you'll never
look into the mouth of death,
that darker paradise?

Then I left you like a skylark
charmed by her own song
though for many years I was afraid
of my reflection. We moved away
to our own cursed cities with sparks
for eyes, smoke for hands.

I heard you met a stranger
who led you by the neck
to yourself-on-your-knees
in the gray morning.
I met a man who shook my shoulders
till they fell like blossoms
when the rain came.
I could hear your pulse
although I was heartless.
It coursed through me like trade winds
through a southern cave.

Once when we were young
you made circles on my back
when the spirit returned
and demons made shapes
across the ceiling at dusk.
I knew death had eyes that were lidless.
But you locked your gaze there
so that I could be free.
This is how you came
and taught me how to pray.
You took one look
and could not stop looking.

PRESENT IN ALL THINGS

In New York, summers sank into us like a hot tire and winters cut deep
so we'd walk arm-in-arm for a cup of warmth
our faces wrapped in snow. Now I live in a seasonless city

and I don't know where I am, or how, or what month.
My grandmother who's dead is telling me stories
and my sister's saying I'm going to die young

and last night I yelled at a cop in West Oakland while his partner
looked on, my tremulous rage spiking the air around us
with burnt cinnamon. What I mean to say is: I'm living.

What I mean to say is: Sometimes I can taste my own madness
and I don't mind it, and I miss you, and I'm alive.
When explaining immanence to my students I say

Immanence means everything is both sacred and equal
at the same time, do you know how revolutionary this is?
History teaches us otherwise. History has taught you

to tie a black ribbon tight around your throat and try singing
and to do this every morning and call it good.
Do you remember the tipping hill town we passed

on our drive to the coast? The one with the dusk light
cut from a vein and the warm bread at midnight
and a dependable land line but no hot water

and no spare devices for cooling? In my dreams we arrive there
and we park the car forever. Then we sit like two children
at the top of a stopped Ferris wheel and tell each other everything.

Tree of Life

Maybe you're in a place I've never been
say Michigan. It's summer. Poplars throbbing green
all around you. Maybe she's a Leo

and she's standing in your driveway
with her breasts like the gospel
and her hot gold hoops. Or maybe she's a Cancer

and you're the kid in chemistry
staring out the window, dreaming
of a queen. Writing her a letter

in your blue jay mind: her of the homecoming.
Her of the deep thoughts. Her pale new body
keeping safe an old soul at seventeen. And didn't

you love her. Didn't you try. Didn't you find her
standing in your driveway on a Tuesday night
beneath a cracked blue dusk when she was perfect

for the last time. Her of the wild. Her
of the father. Her before the tree of life. Before
she was prey. Didn't you love her

in your silent way—listening to everything
she could think of to say to you
until her voice made a home for you
and the world went dark.

SPRING, SAN FRANCISCO

for Gabriel

You live in a house of sound and you live
with a ghost. The one who stole your heart
also lives in your heart so you cut it out
with a carving knife and send it flying.
You say sometimes you wake and wait
for the god of loneliness to leave you alone.
I say our city is small and teeming
with ghosts and there are no seasons
for hiding. So we let go of the ones
who called us by our names. We make
ourselves new names by tracing letters
in a sand tray with sharp stones.
This is called Patience or Practicing
Solitude or The Wind Will Ruin Everything
but what does it matter let's go for beauty
every time. You say the price we pay for love
is loss. I say the price we pay for love
is love. Sometimes you've nothing
save your hand in the glove and the glove
against wind and you're jabbing at the sky now
in the match of your life but the sky
never fights back so you praise it.

Summer, San Buenaventura

You wake.

A small but growing

addiction to dawn

at your throat's hollow.

Days by the sea were once few

and far between

now your mornings are a tide

of vanishing starlight

over bone white sand.

What has pulled away

will continue to return.

What you can't remember

you praise.

WINTER, ITHACA

Tonight I walk out into winter's fingers
stepping from one stone

and onto another,
the stones receding into darkness

as I leave them. Smoke from a home fire
roams the air. Snow comes.

My shoulders go soft—
two blades loosening into the spine—

and for once I'm a witness,
not a careless warrior, who watches the leaves

as they turn and die, and Jon
is leaving. Lynn is lying

about her life, so I can't help her.
I'm miles away

so I can't hold her or hold her down.
But what is the cold

compared to the fire?
Where does the rage go?

The road's packed with snow.
Black tea steams

between my hands and I drink it down
until it burns.

Autumn in the Garden
With Her Ghost

She said *Find me in the garden*
so I followed her wish
to the end of the light.

She was sitting like a woman
who's been sitting on a cold slab
for many ages. Her hair was white

and her hands were spotted
in the way they were spotted
when I was young. I said, "I'm afraid

to let go of the world."
She lifted a black stone
from the shallow pond

and palmed it—*You think*
that I'm asking
for you to renounce it.

I said, "I believe
that beauty is power.
Look how the ash tree

catches the light;
look at the jasmine."
I watched as she closed

her fist around the stone
then opened it. A bright emptiness
thrummed there.

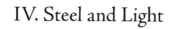

IV. Steel and Light

PROLOGUE

My childhood? Yes—

Pears in the summer,
mini-blinds drawn against a midday heat,

falling off a bike, forehead to brick,
scratching at the stitches

and the marvelous voices—
how they chimed in the night

speaking in the dark space
between my eyes—

Listen: they've returned—

[MOONLIGHT]

I pour through the portal of your window.
See how you do that?
Twist your torso to lie beneath my light?

Betrayal is a killer;
you should've died
when he spoke her name

or tipped into ether
from the pull of desire
when he told you

but you didn't.
You held firm
to the wood floor

while something within you tumbled down a ridge
then rose in an instant
to stroke him.

Like a god
you forgave him—
for how else without him

could you know the world?
You think your chest
is full of weeds.

I think if you cracked half your rib
and rubbed it dry
a man might emerge—

you are that lonely.

[Gun]

Every time you hold me
you have a choice.

What will you ruin?
Will you deign to choose deliverance

or, like a witness

will you die by your own hand
for the beauty here?

[Knife]

You took me in your right hand—

Then took me in your left—

Years later, you rub stems
across your scars, as if such marks
were carved in sand.

What did you learn
from your first act of violence?

That the body is a door
to be entered by a soul, grazing the edges
of the cuts you made?

That the body is a cage,
unlit and guarded by the fastening eye?

Or maybe that the body is a threshold
to freedom—
a startling freedom you've craved since creation—

and I am your tool
of first resort.

[STAR]

So. You've returned to the water of first searching
searcher that you are
to burn beneath our burning.

What could you be wondering,
crouched on the outskirts, breathing steam
from a winter river?

When you were first born
you shuddered in the darkness, unable
to stand it: the vastness—

a land without rootstalk, tree stem,
or rain storm, lacking
reflection. You held forth

in our garden of absence
till it threw you downward, towards a world
without light.

No one knew you and the creatures drowned you
with their dark displays
of human love. So you became

like us: everywhere at once
and always departing.

But the river's laughter, like winter,
is holy—and you are more eternal
than you think.

[TRACKS]

Come down here. Crouch on the cold. How serious
do you imagine your life to be? Indeed,
it is serious—a steel thing

couldn't break your will, now could it.
Inside you is a kernel
that can never be killed, if you

could believe it. Not even I
or the train across my back
could crush it.

[First Daylight]

If you were a monk would it be any better?
Yesterday you took your skull
for a walk. Thinking about emptiness

and the lottery of pain
you stood in the book aisles, breathing
like a broken tulip. Look, said the masters,

there's nowhere more cancerous
than your arrogant heart.
Well! Balling your bitter into fists

like a child, you threw the last of your goodness
under foot. No salt now in the May heat.
No green in the summer valley.

Well be near me, I'm breaking
over the eastern seas. Soon you'll be running
to the edge of the city to see me leave.

Coda: Deep in the Cloud-filled Valley

You will never return
to your mother's house
or your father's garden

and the bed of your husband
will whittle away.

What sort of life is that?
Leaving things
so as to praise them later
with your own strangeness.

Now you think I won't know you
from the clouds that surround you
but you exalt everything
that cannot contain you—

I'll know you by your joy.

NOTES

The Gathering Mind: "We are helped in the shedding of dominant kinship groups by the relative individualism of the Angles and Saxons," is from Robin Fox's essay, "The Kindness of Strangers," reprinted in *Harper's Magazine*, October 2007.

The Gathering Mind: "I cannot muster the 'we' except by finding the way in which I am tied to you . . . My own language must break up and yield if I am to know you," is from Judith Butler's *Precarious Life: Violence, Mourning, and Politics*. New York, London: Verso, 2004, p. 49.